JOURNEY ACROSS THE ARCTIC

by Sheila Sweeny Higginson
illustrated by Tamara English

Scott Foresman
is an imprint of

Glenview, Illinois • Boston, Massachusetts • Chandler, Arizona
Upper Saddle River, New Jersey

Illustrators
3-19 Tamara English; **20** Dan Trush

ISBN 13: 978-0-328-51365-9
ISBN 10:   0-328-51365-2

10 11 12 13 V0FL 17 16 15 14

The Arctic is an extreme place. It is extremely cold. It is extremely far away. It is extremely dangerous. It is the perfect spot for an extreme adventure.

Very few people attempt to cross the Arctic because of the harsh conditions. But those conditions were exactly what made Luca and Serena Cullen head straight for the North Pole as soon as the opportunity came along. The brother-and-sister adventure team had become renowned around the world for their incredible adventuring. Now they longed to tackle the most intense challenge they could imagine—traveling across the Arctic to the North Pole in the deadly dark of winter.

Ever since they were children, Luca and Serena had spent most of their time dreaming of adventures. As a boy, Luca loved to set off on snowshoe hikes through the mountains near their home in the Alps of Europe. It wasn't long before his little sister, Serena, tagged along behind him.

It seemed as if Luca and Serena were born to be the perfect extreme team. Luca was the planner. He was organized, responsible, and efficient. Serena was the dreamer. She had the true spirit of an adventurer. If Luca said that an expedition was impossible, Serena was sure to convince him that they could handle the challenge.

Their physical skills also complemented each other. Luca was a powerful skier. He could forge a trail through any snowdrift he encountered. Serena was an equally capable swimmer. She said that she could feel a burst of energy explode from her body as soon as her fingertips hit the water. Together, they believed they could overcome any obstacle nature put in their path.

When they were older, the siblings' first real expedition was a trek across the frozen ice fields of Patagonia in South America. On this trip, they learned that a successful adventure required two key ingredients: thorough planning and rigorous training.

They agreed that Luca would be responsible for planning all of their future missions. He raised money to fund each adventure by sending letters to potential sponsors. He determined what supplies they would need for each trip, such as a medical kit, an insulated tent, and an inflatable raft. He arranged emergency rescue squads that could be summoned by a radio, and he always carried a global positioning system (GPS). The hand-held GPS receiver gave the siblings their exact location—no matter how remote they were.

Serena organized their training camp. She and her brother dragged heavy tires up snowy hills so they'd be able to pull sleds loaded with equipment. They ran countless miles to prepare for long, exhausting days.

For several years, Luca and Serena traveled around the world. They climbed mountains and journeyed in places few people had ever seen before. With each expedition, they tested the limits of their bodies and their minds.

One day, back at home, Serena was reading the newspaper when a headline caught her attention. "Listen to this," she called to her brother. "Kevin and John Wilson are trying to make a name for themselves. They are planning to be the first sibling team to travel across the Arctic to the North Pole—in *winter*."

"Good luck to them," Luca replied. "That's a risky mission."

Serena held the paper in front of her brother's face. "You're not getting it, Luca," she said. "They are *planning* a mission. They haven't done it yet. That means that we could get there first!"

"Are you sure you're awake?" Luca asked.

"Why?" Serena replied.

"Because you must be dreaming to think we could cross the Arctic during winter!

Do you know what that would mean?" Luca laughed.

But every day for the next week, Serena taunted her brother. "Kevin Wilson must think he's a better planner than you," she said.

"He's not," Luca answered.

"Maybe John's become a stronger skier?" Serena questioned.

"Doubtful," Luca replied.

"You know what really gets to me?" Serena asked him one day.

"I have no idea," Luca said.

"The fact that they're making a big deal about being the first *brothers* to travel across the Arctic in winter. Wouldn't it be an even better story if there were a *woman* involved?"

At that, Luca smiled. He knew his fate was sealed. That night they began planning for their most dangerous adventure yet.

The trip *was* very dangerous. The first night, Luca heard the growls of a polar bear. He knew that the bear could rip through their tent with one swipe of a paw. He also knew it would happily eat up all of their food supply.

"Get the flare gun," Luca called. "We need to chase that bear away now!"

"I'm on it, Luca," Serena replied, as she shot a flare into the dark sky. The polar bear lumbered off into the distance.

The adventurers had known they would face bitter cold in the Arctic. Winter temperatures frequently fell below -30°F. They also were prepared for the biting winds that gusted at more than 40 miles per hour.

But it was the darkness—the complete and utter darkness—that Luca and Serena found most difficult to get used to.

People who live in places like Europe and the United States watch as winter eats up daylight hours. But that is nothing compared with what winter does to the daylight hours in the Arctic region around the North Pole. In early October, sunlight disappears, and it doesn't return until early March. During those months, the region is in complete darkness. Luca and Serena had to ski in the dark, eat in the dark, and listen for polar bears in the dark. It was an enormous obstacle on an already challenging path.

On a map or globe, it appears that a person could just hike or ski across a snowy field of Arctic ice to get to the North Pole. But this is not completely true. There are times when the Arctic Ocean freezes all the way to shore. There are other times, however, when it does not, and explorers have to make their way through patches of unstable ice and open water.

That's just what Serena and Luca had to do. There was no solid path they could take to get from Cape Arkticheskiy, Siberia, where their journey began, to the North Pole. They used their skis as much as they could, pulling their equipment behind them. Many times, they skied for nine or ten hours a day. Sometimes they would come to a vast break in the ice. Then they had to use an inflatable raft to get from one ice field to another.

As Luca and Serena were trudging across the Arctic in the second month of their journey, a series of disasters struck. First, a severe storm hit, making it impossible for them to ski anywhere. For several days, they had to stay inside their tent, hoping the storm would not get so bad that they would need to be rescued. Serena was impatient. Luca was worried. He wasn't sure that their food supplies would last. He also was worried that spring would dawn before they reached the North Pole.

When they finally were able to resume their expedition, Luca noticed that something didn't seem right with Serena.

"What's wrong, Sis?"

"Nothing," she said brightly. "I'm fine."

Luca wasn't fooled. He knew his sister better than anyone else on the planet, and he could tell that she was struggling to keep the pace. He knew that Serena wouldn't slow down unless something serious held her back.

Serena was actually in serious danger of ending their trip. A few days before, she had twisted her ankle, and it hadn't stopped hurting. Serena had hidden this from her brother because she feared he would cancel the mission.

The third time Serena winced in pain, however, Luca stopped in his tracks.

"Look, Serena," he said sternly. "If you don't tell me what's wrong, I'm calling for emergency help right now."

"It's my ankle," Serena reluctantly admitted. "I think it's sprained."

Luca's first instinct was to yell at her for not telling him sooner. But then he thought about how much pain his sister must be feeling. He set up camp, took out their medical supply kit, and began the process of taping her ankle.

With a bandaged ankle, Serena forced herself to keep going. Luca was concerned about his sister, but he knew that she had made up her mind and would not quit.

Serena's medical condition was not the only thing the pair was worried about. Supplies were running short, and the first light of spring was only a week away!

The pair worked harder than they had ever worked in their lives. Two days before spring, they realized their goal was in sight.

"We're getting close!" Serena exclaimed as she looked at her GPS coordinates. "I think we've still got a shot!"

For the next two days the siblings pushed forward with new motivation. They knew that each step was bringing them closer to their goal. When they finally had the North Pole in their sights, they forgot everything else and sprinted the final meters of the long journey. They had made it while it was still winter!

Serena collapsed and broke down in tears of relief. Luca stood silently for a moment and watched the faint glow of spring slowly brightening the Arctic sky. Then he pulled his sister up and hugged her tightly. They really were born to be the perfect extreme team!

Polar Night

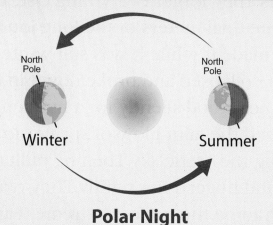

North Pole

Winter

North Pole

Summer

Polar Night

In this story, Serena and Luca trekked across the Arctic for several months in darkness. What the siblings experienced is known as Polar Night.

What causes Polar Night? The diagram shows Earth's path around the sun. During the winter months, the North Pole is tilted away from the sun. The sun's light never reaches the North Pole. As Earth spins, most places on Earth experience daytime and nighttime every 24 hours. But during winter, the North Pole remains in darkness.

Can you guess what happens during the summer months? The North Pole is tilted toward the sun. The North Pole faces the sun 24 hours a day, so it is always daytime. This is called Polar Day, or the Midnight Sun.